Girls in Ancient Asian Fashion

A hand-drawn coloring book

Queenie Wong

ISBN-13 978-1725982239
ISBN-10 1725982234
First published in United States in 2018
All artworks are made by Queenie Wong
Wonger0050@yahoo.com.hk
Copyright 2018 by Queenie Wong
All rights reserved.
No part of this book may be reproduced in any form for commercial used without written permission from the author.

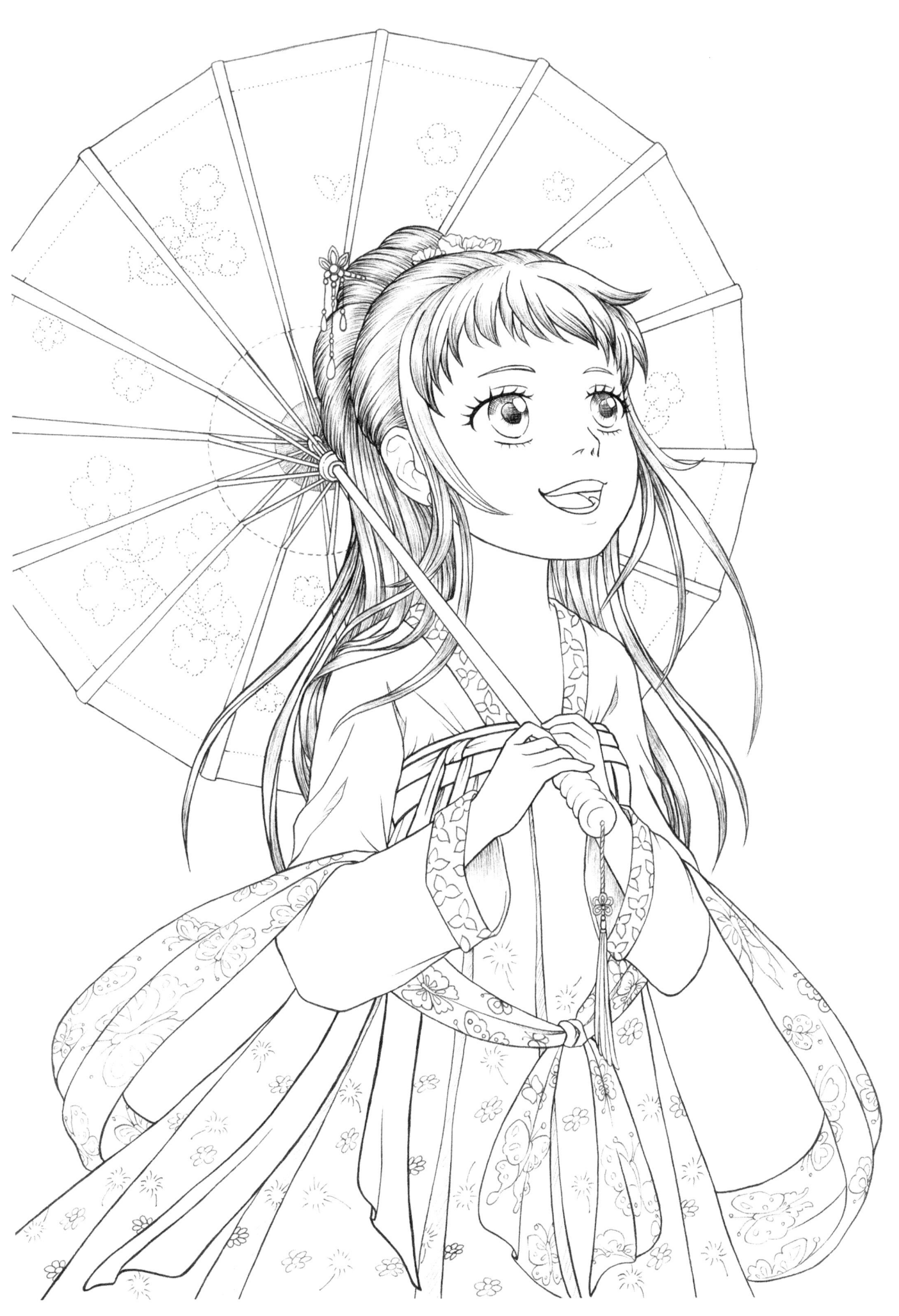

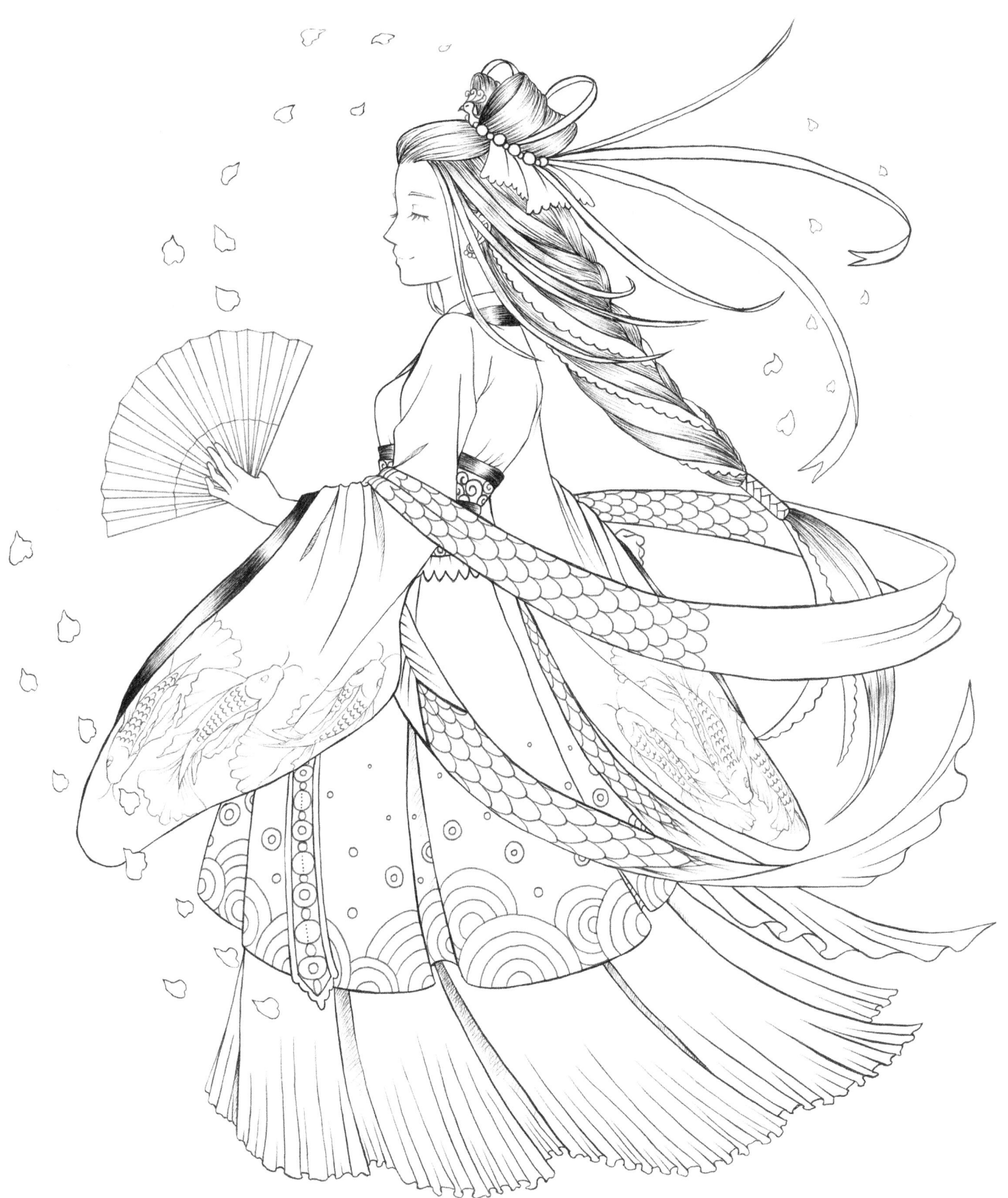

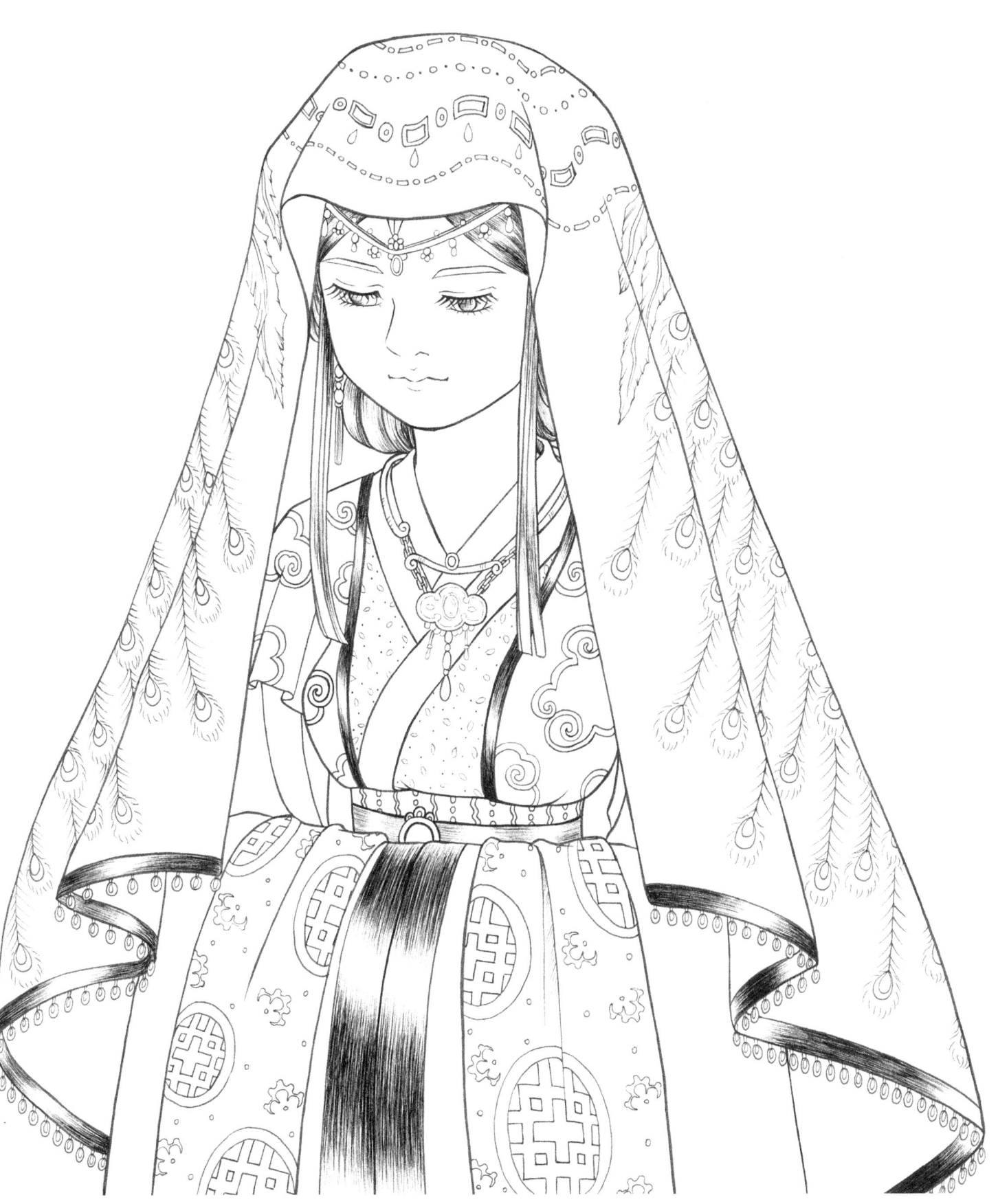

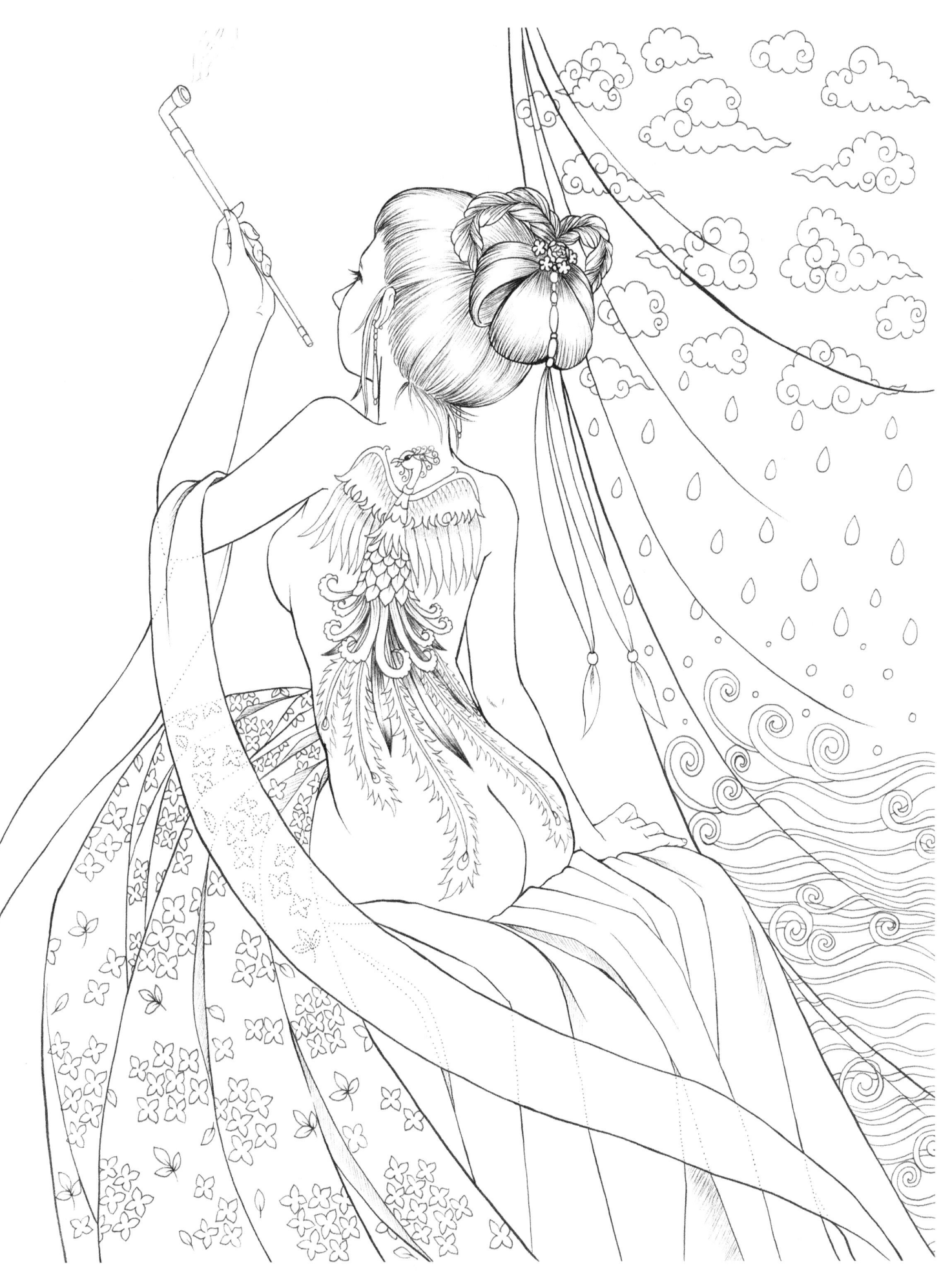

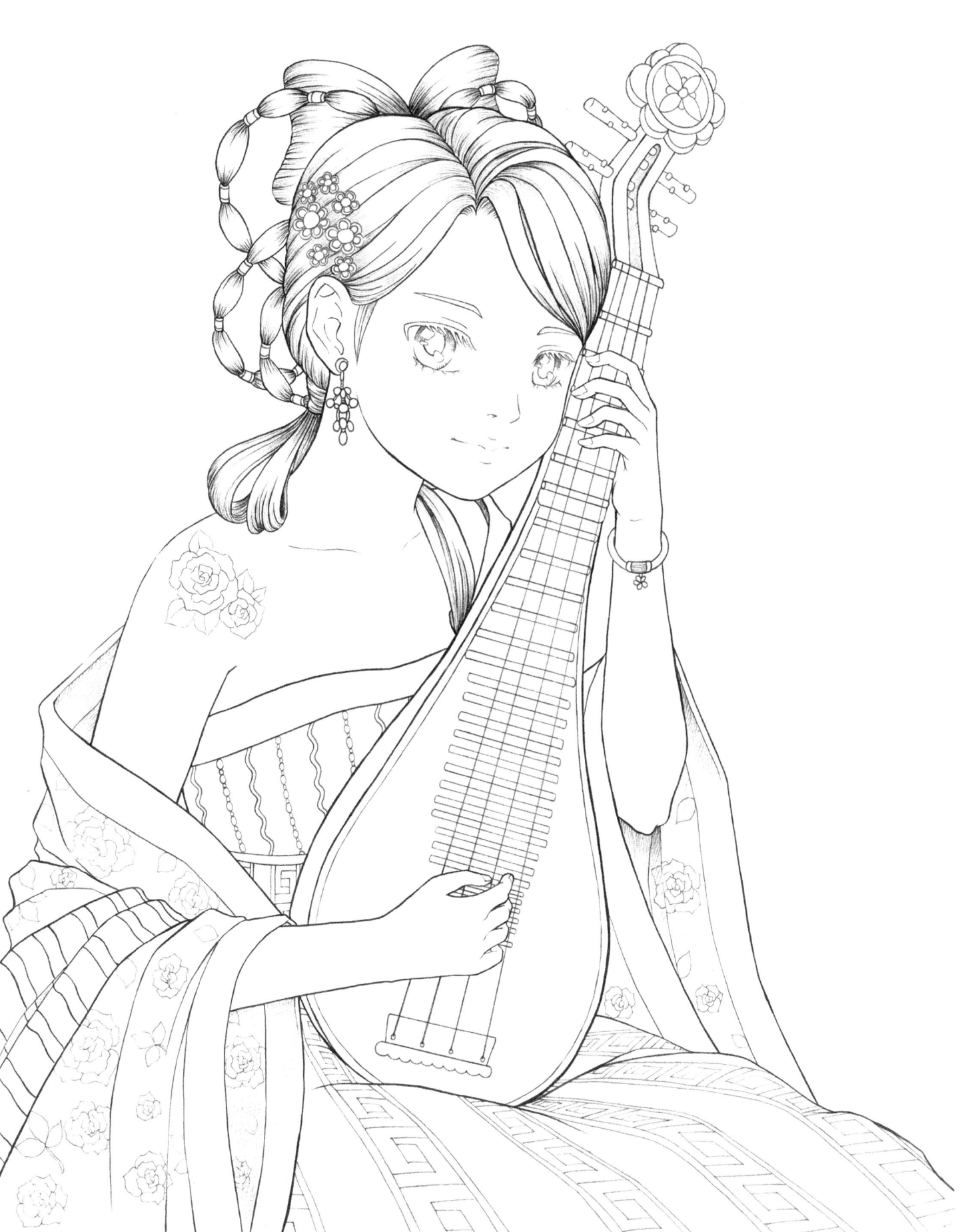

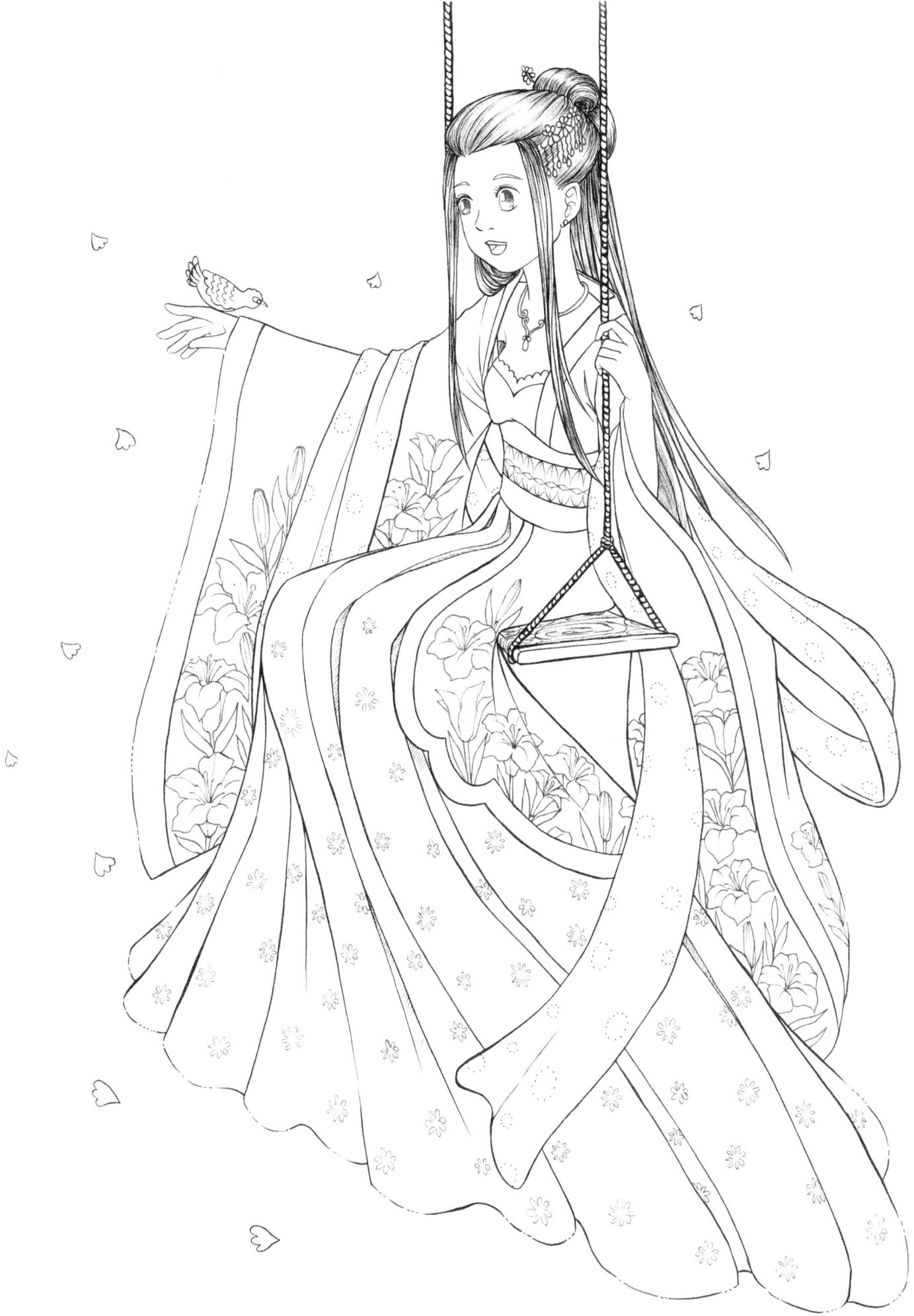

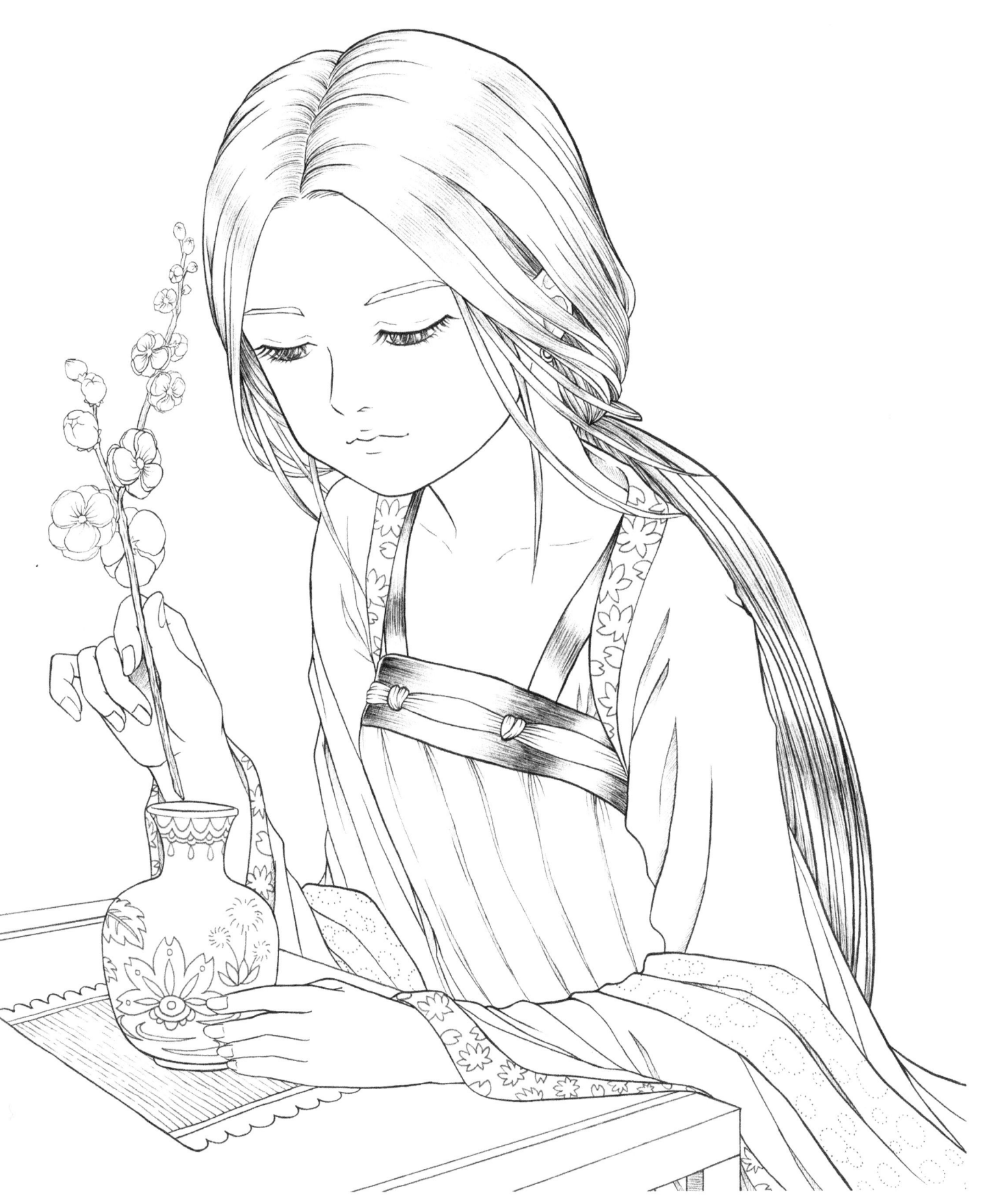

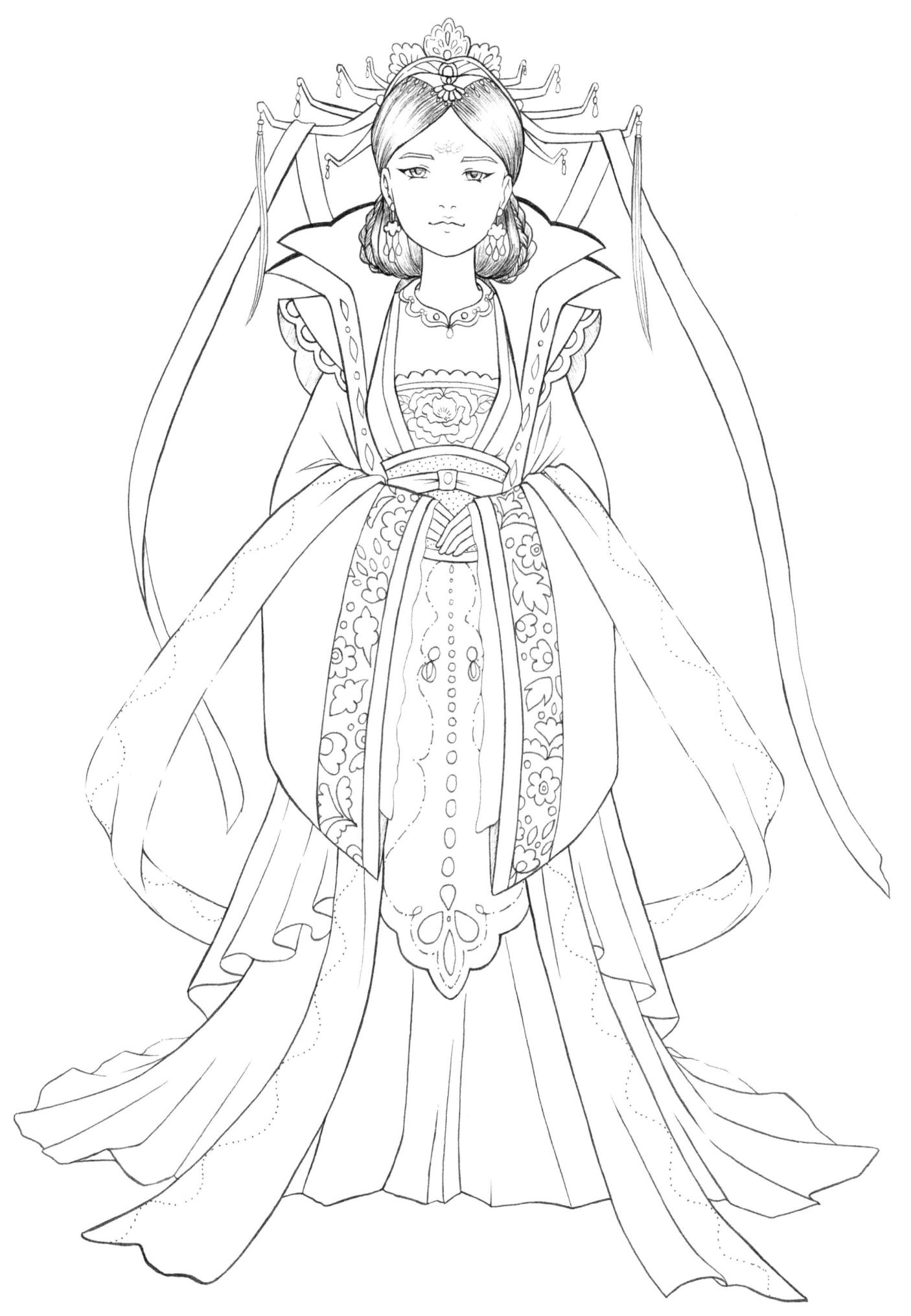

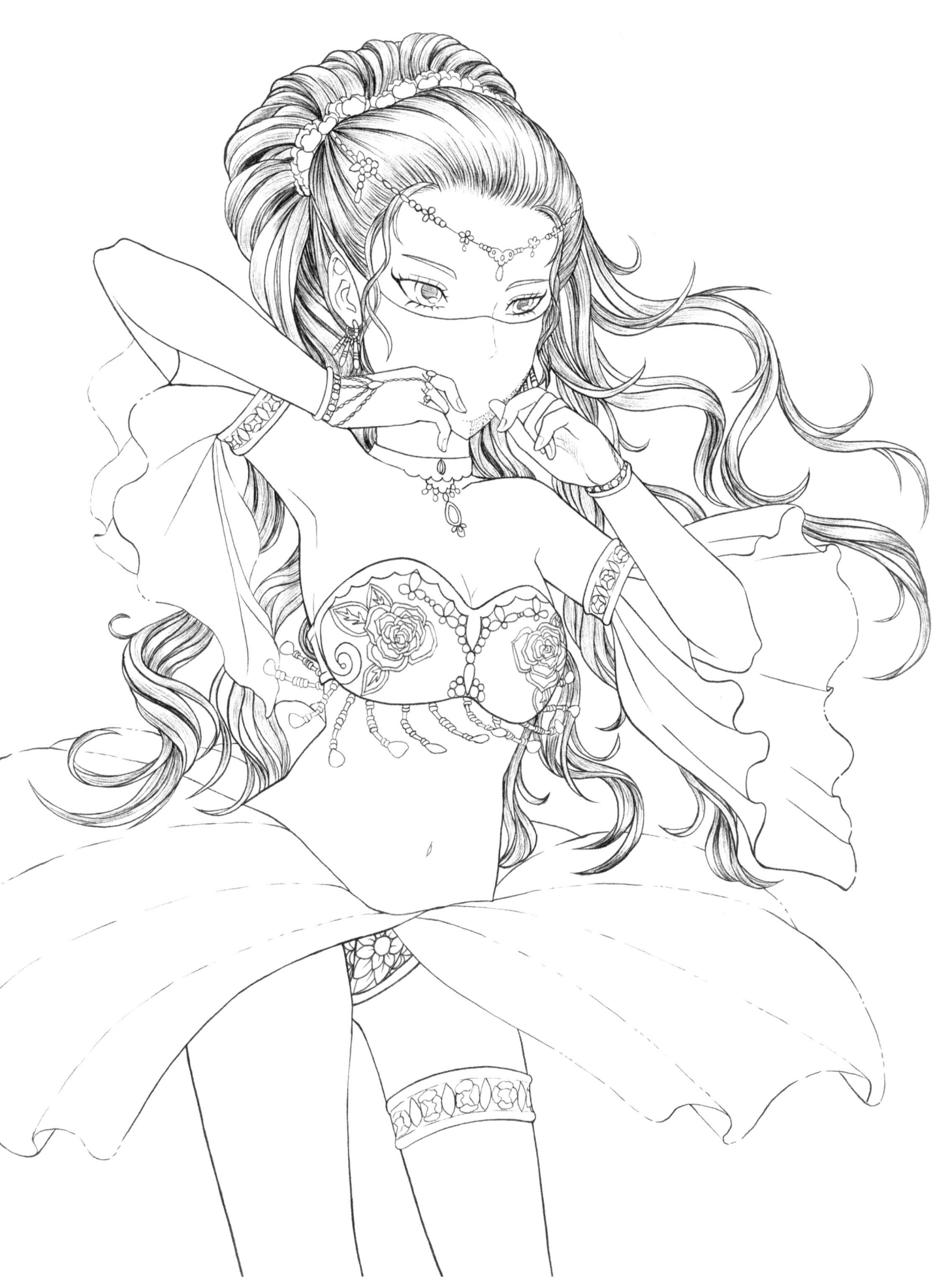

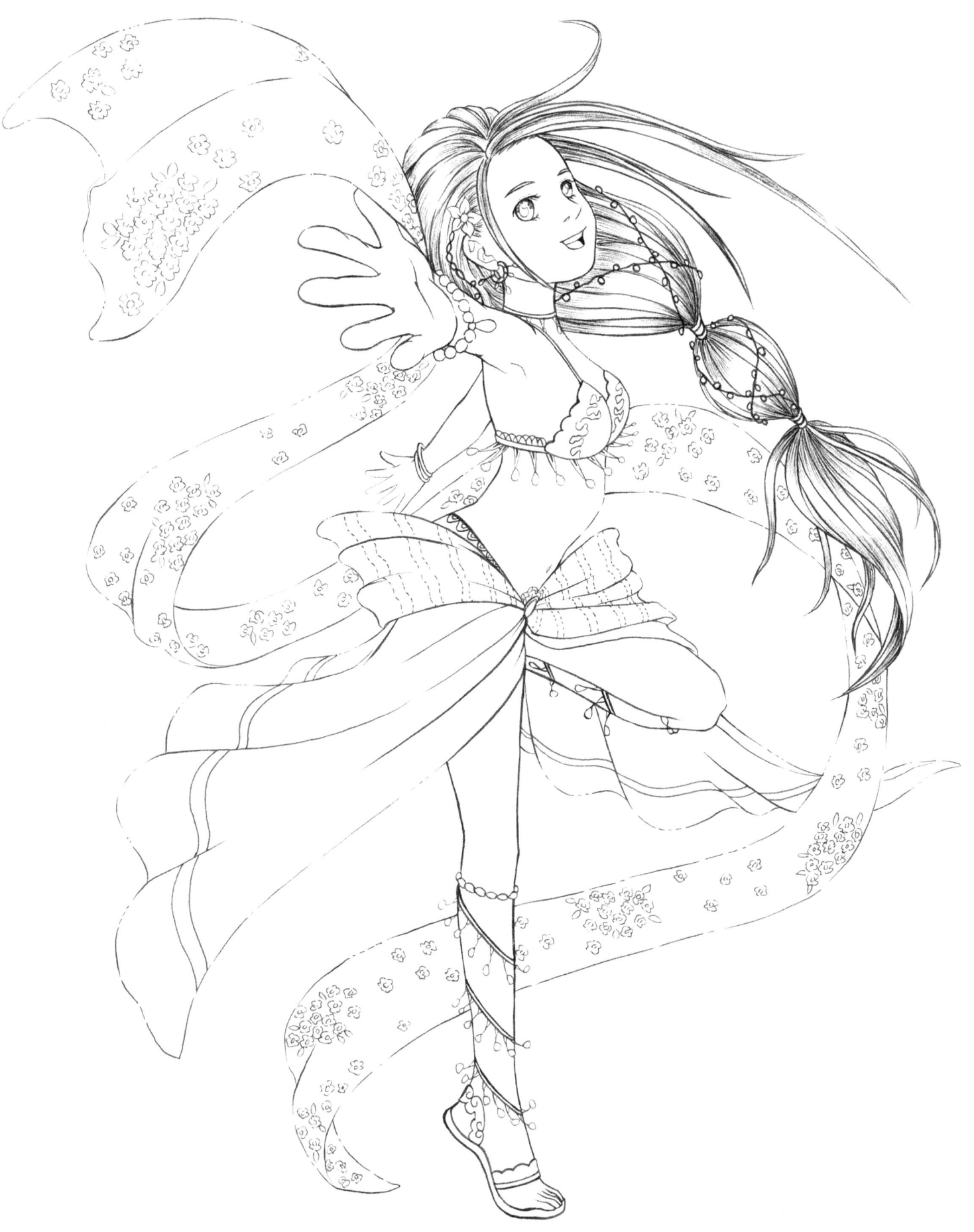

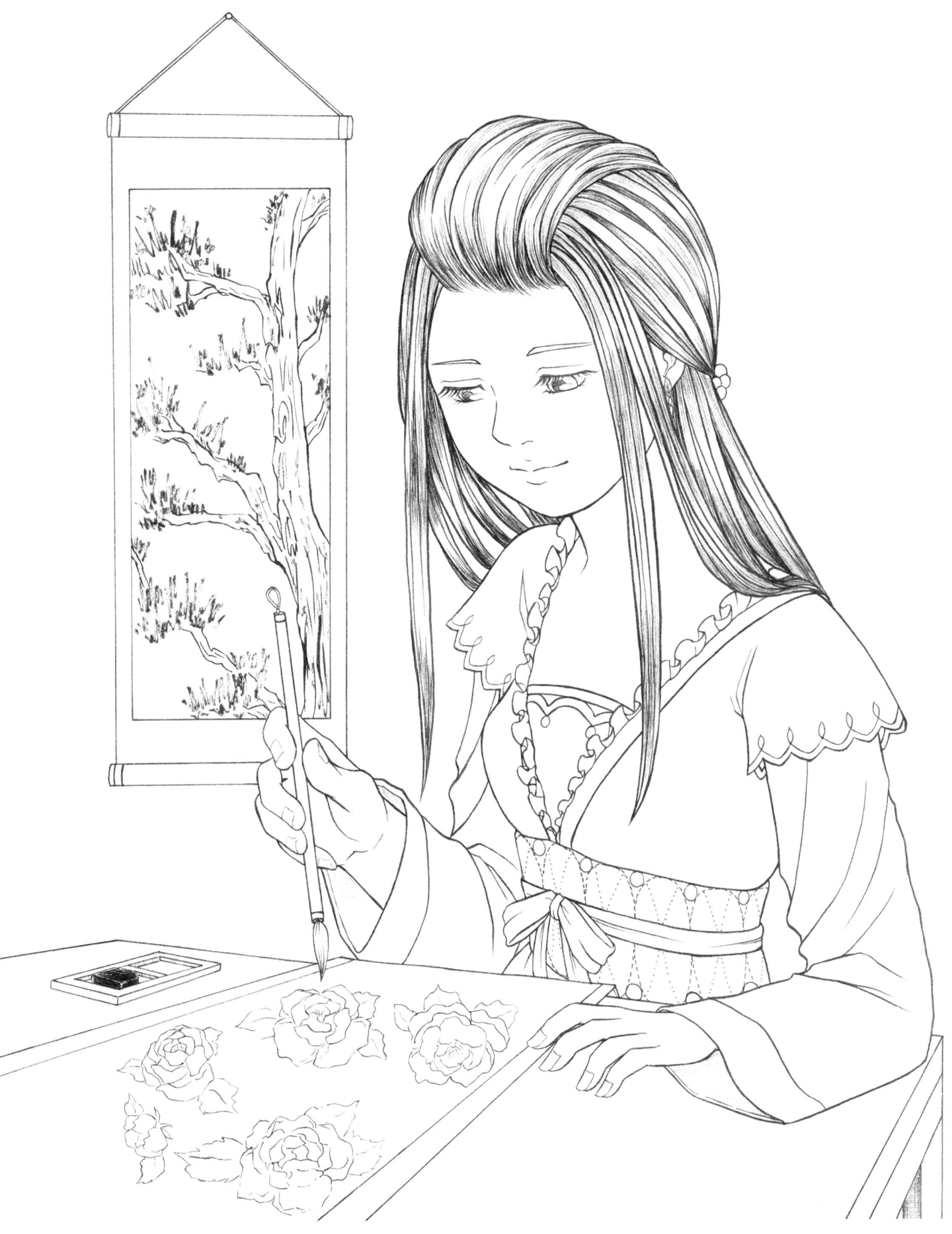

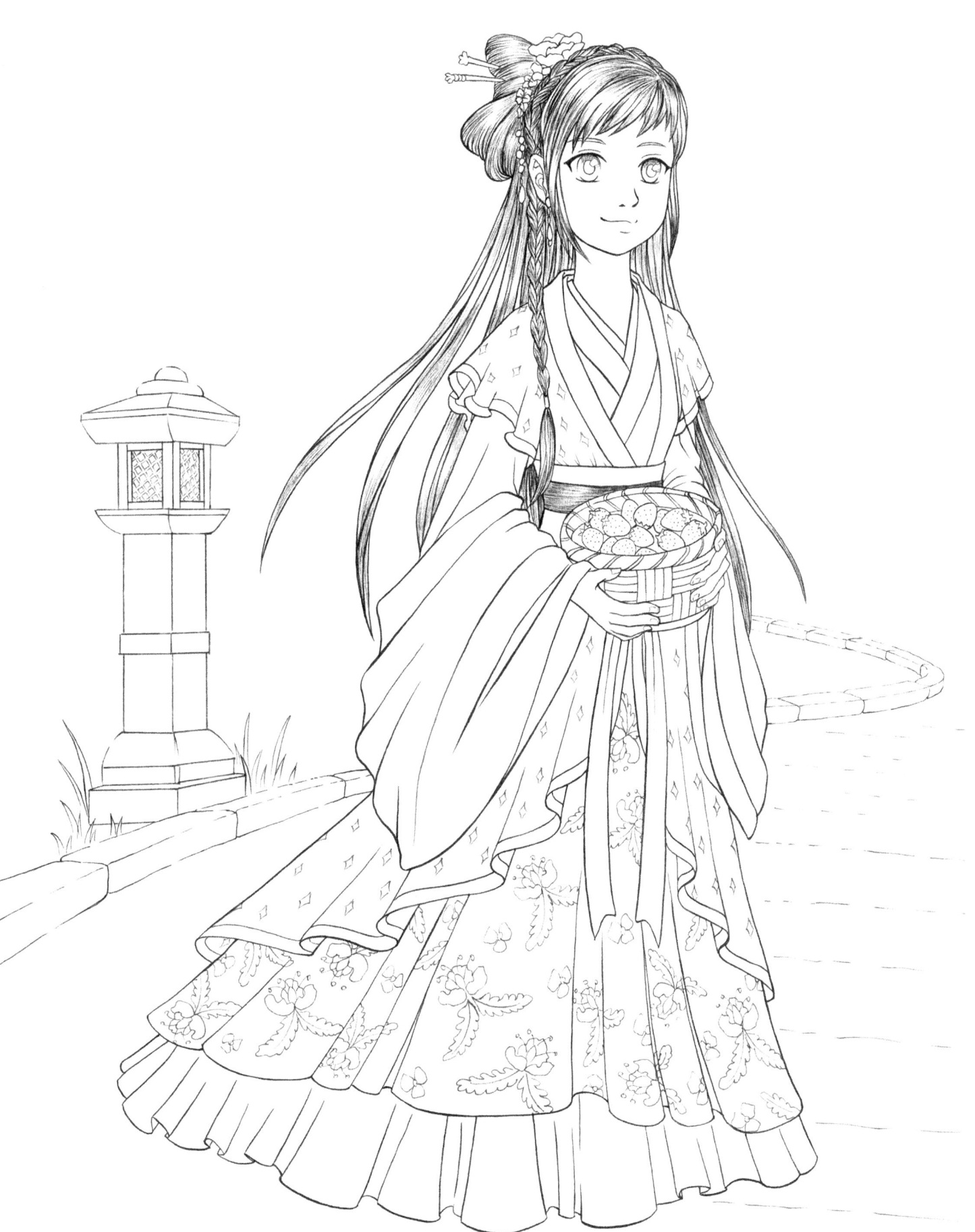

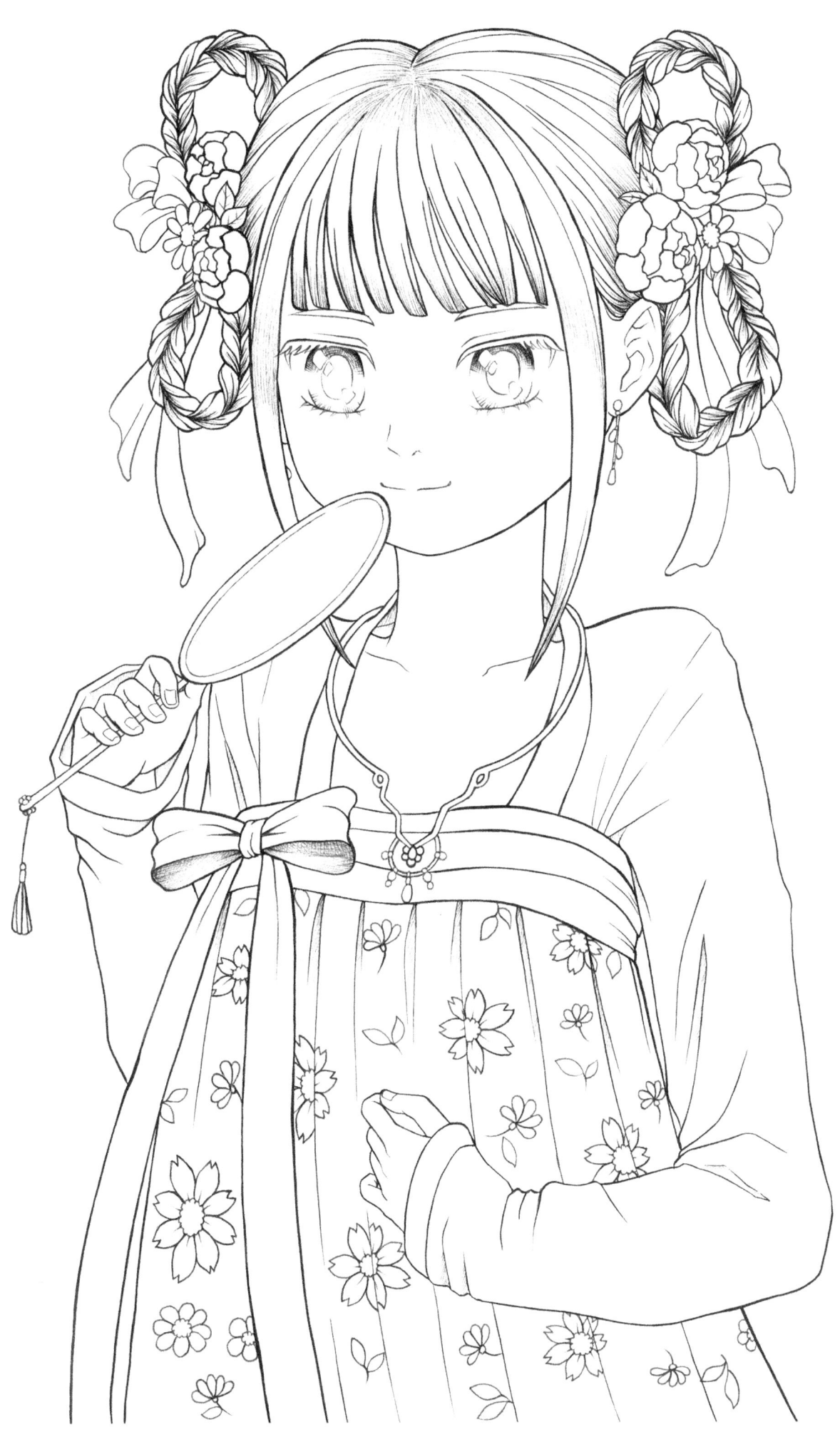

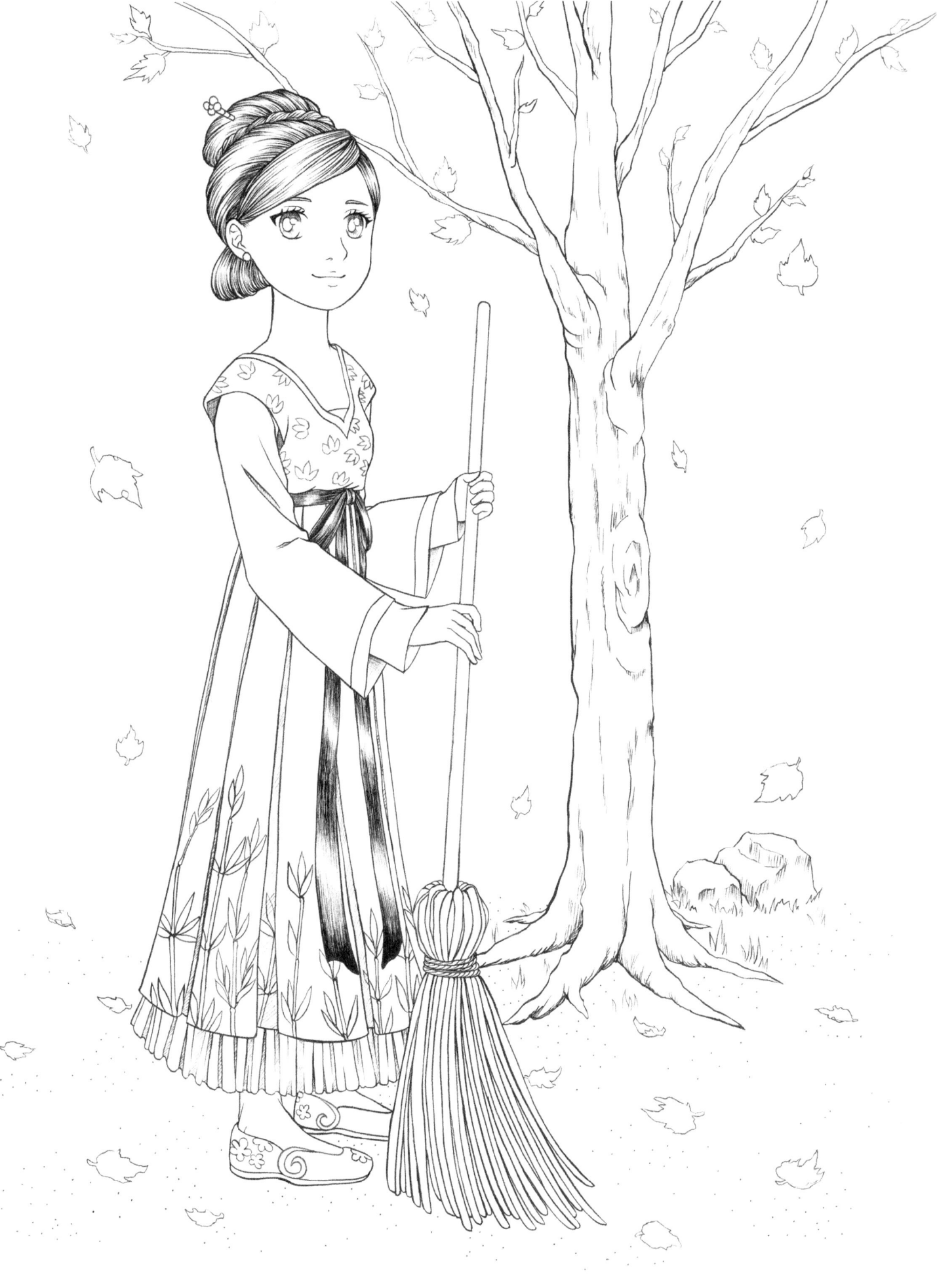

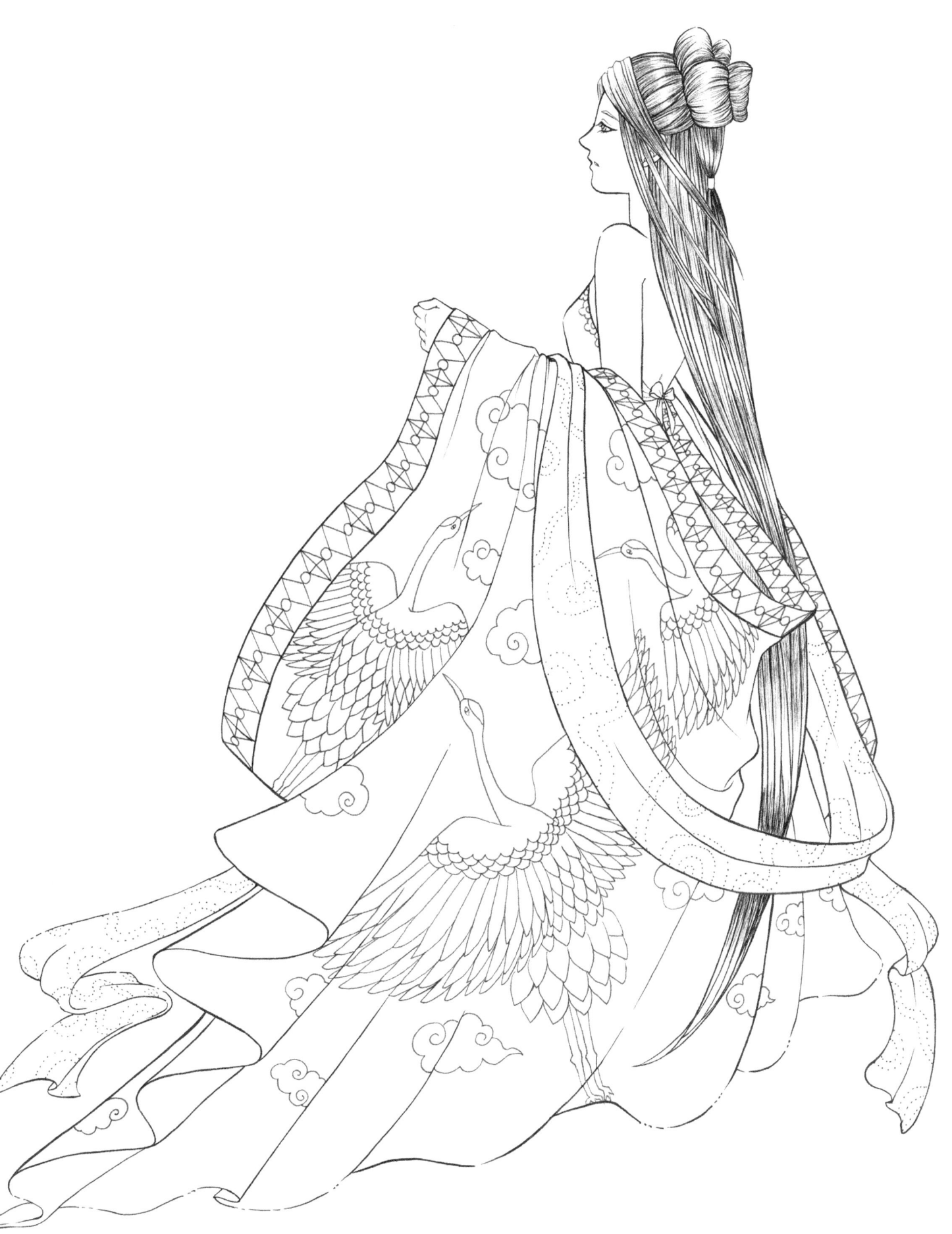

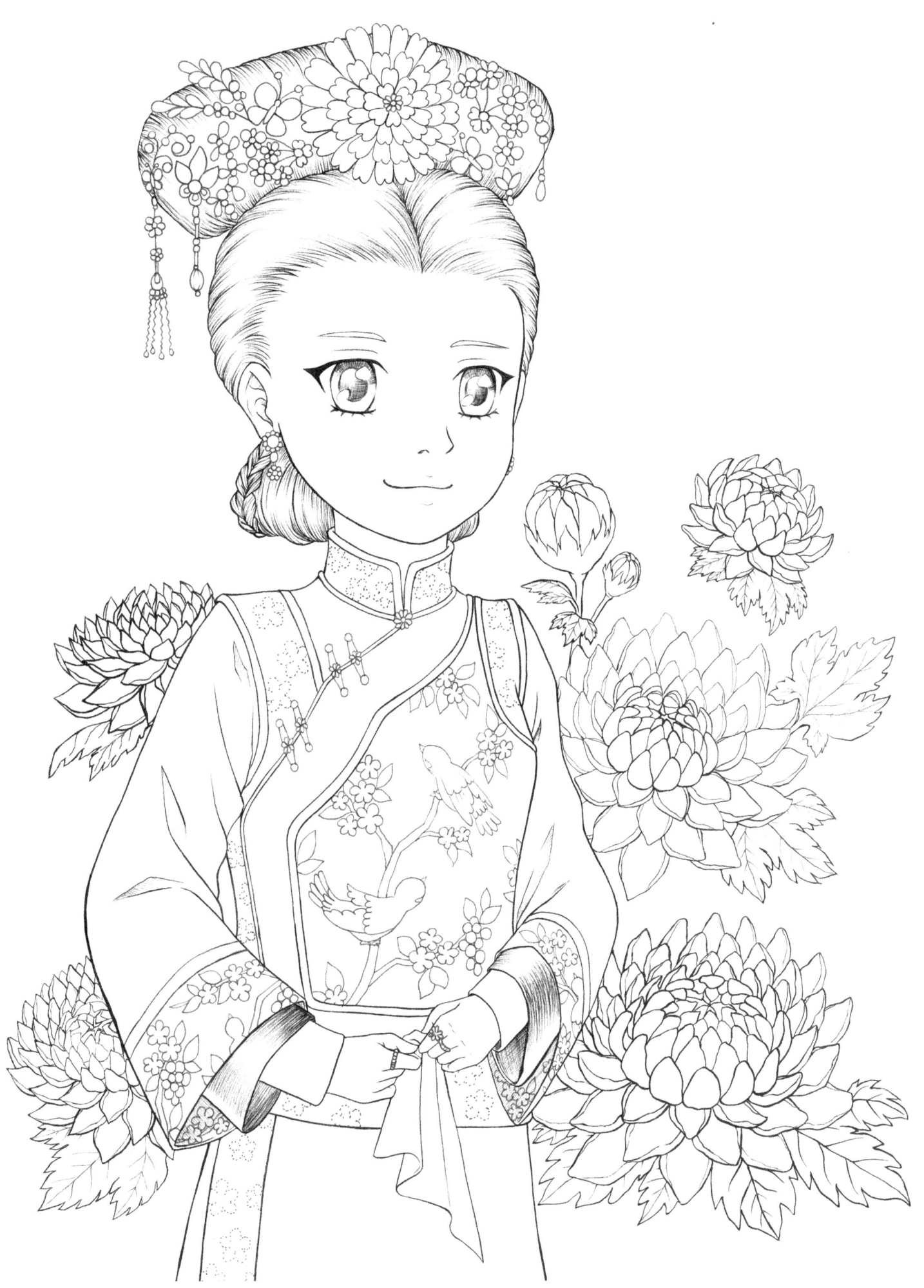

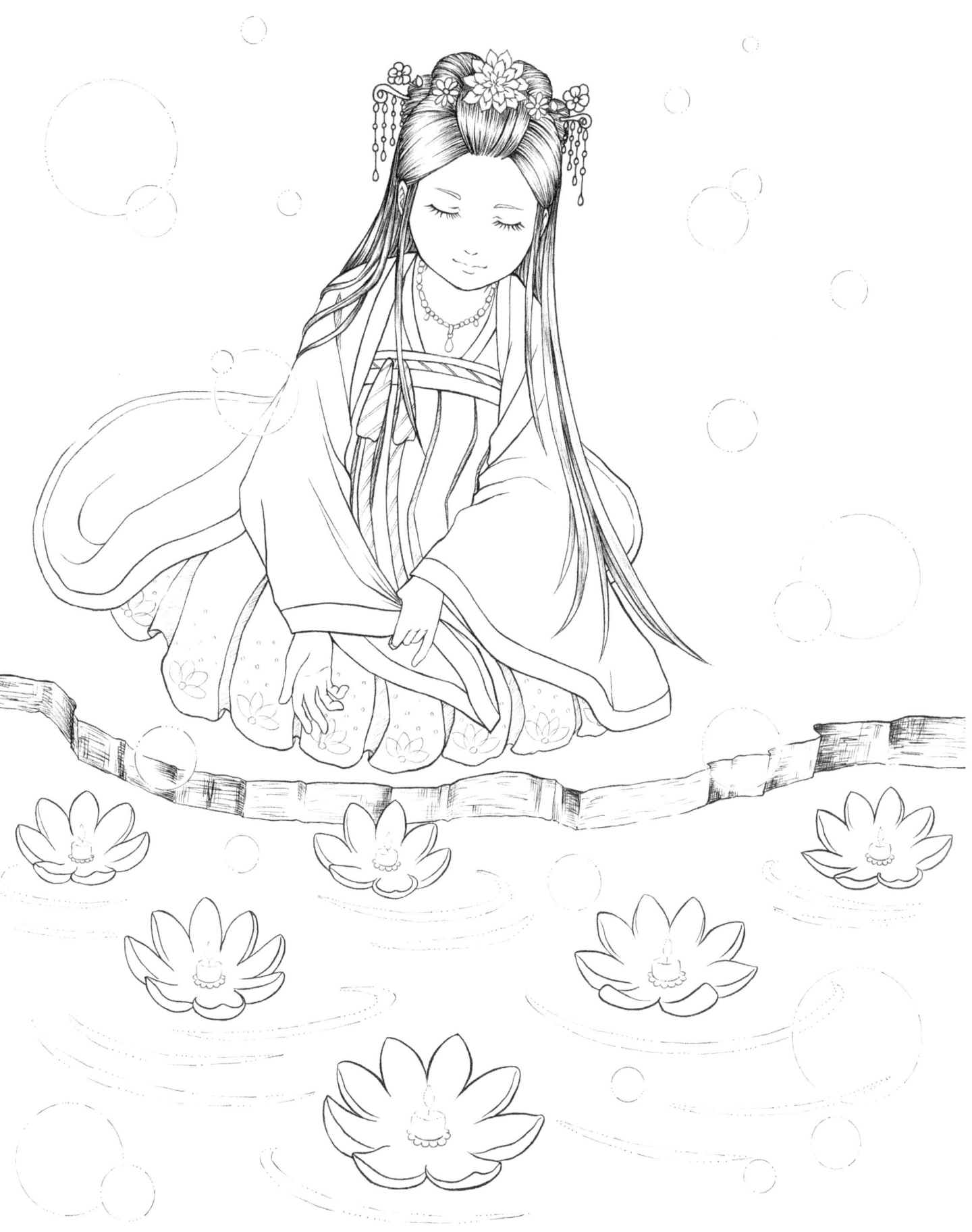

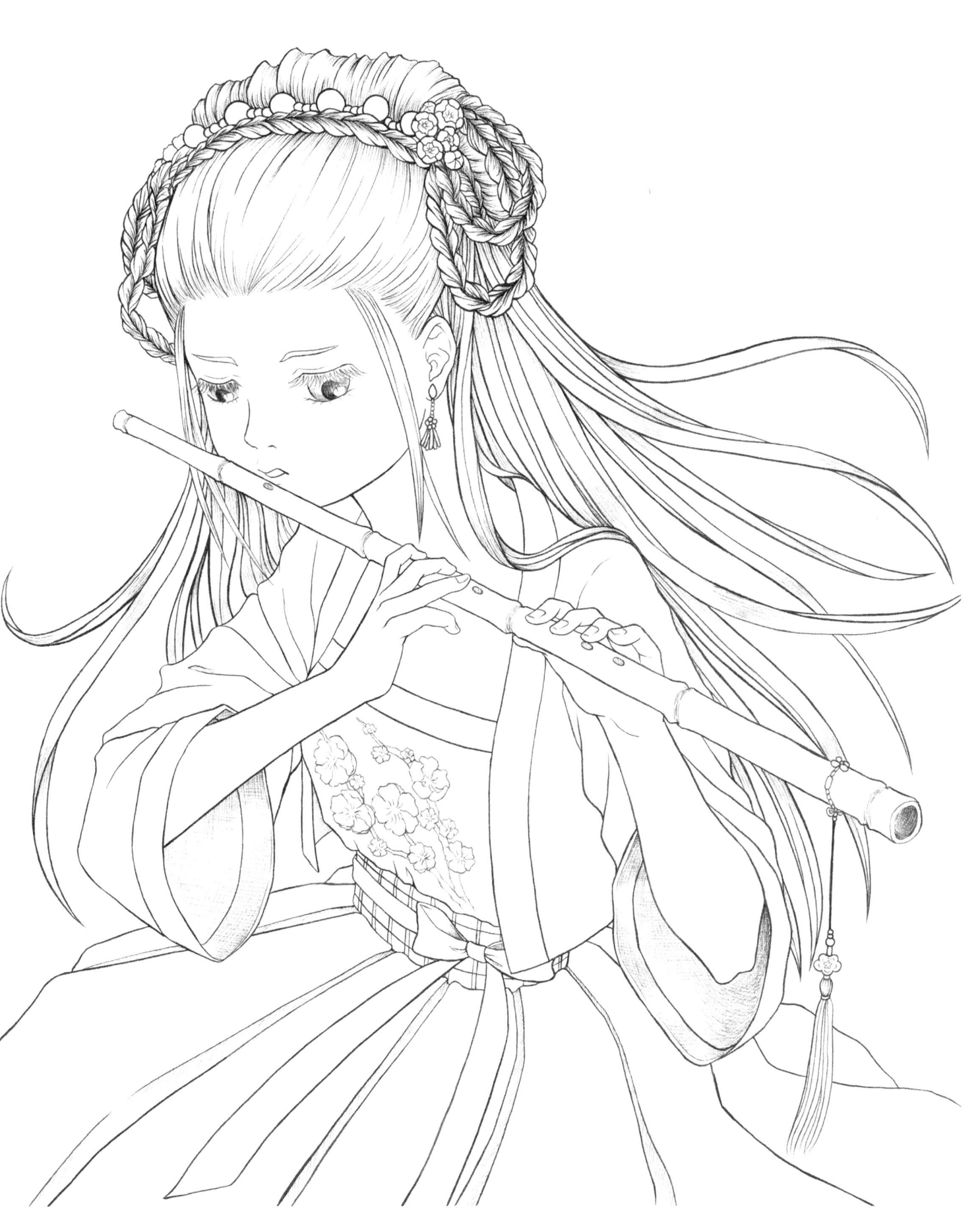

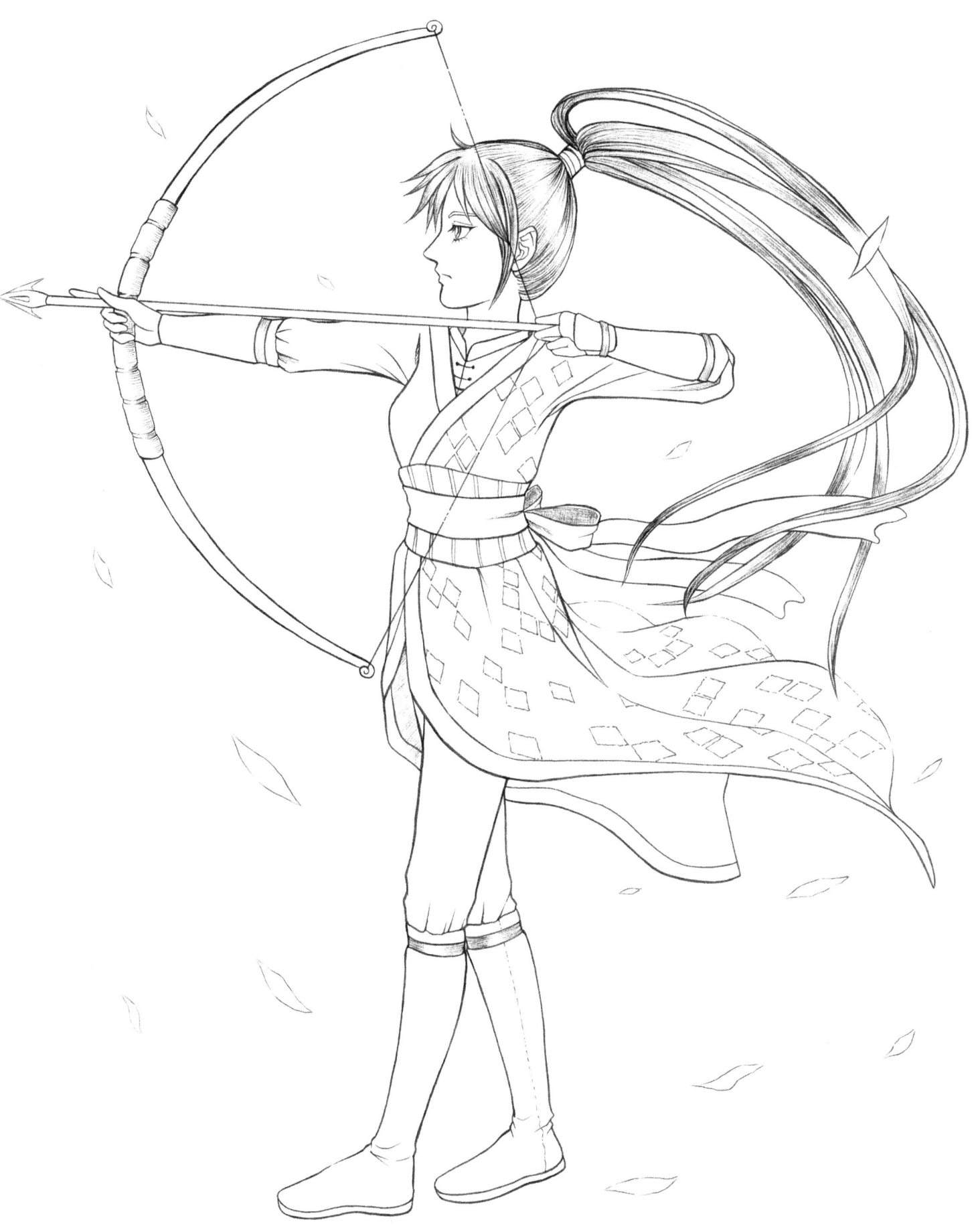

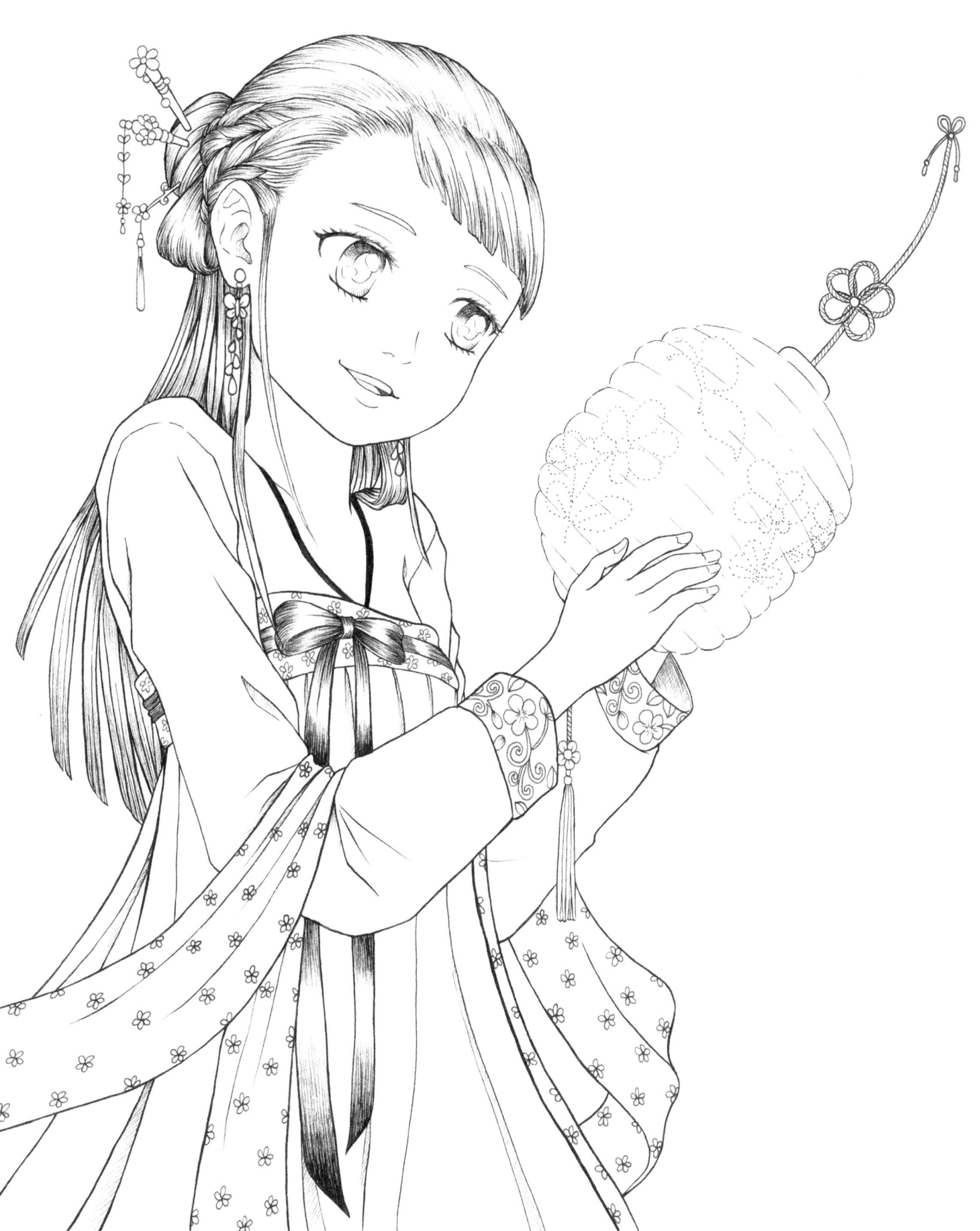

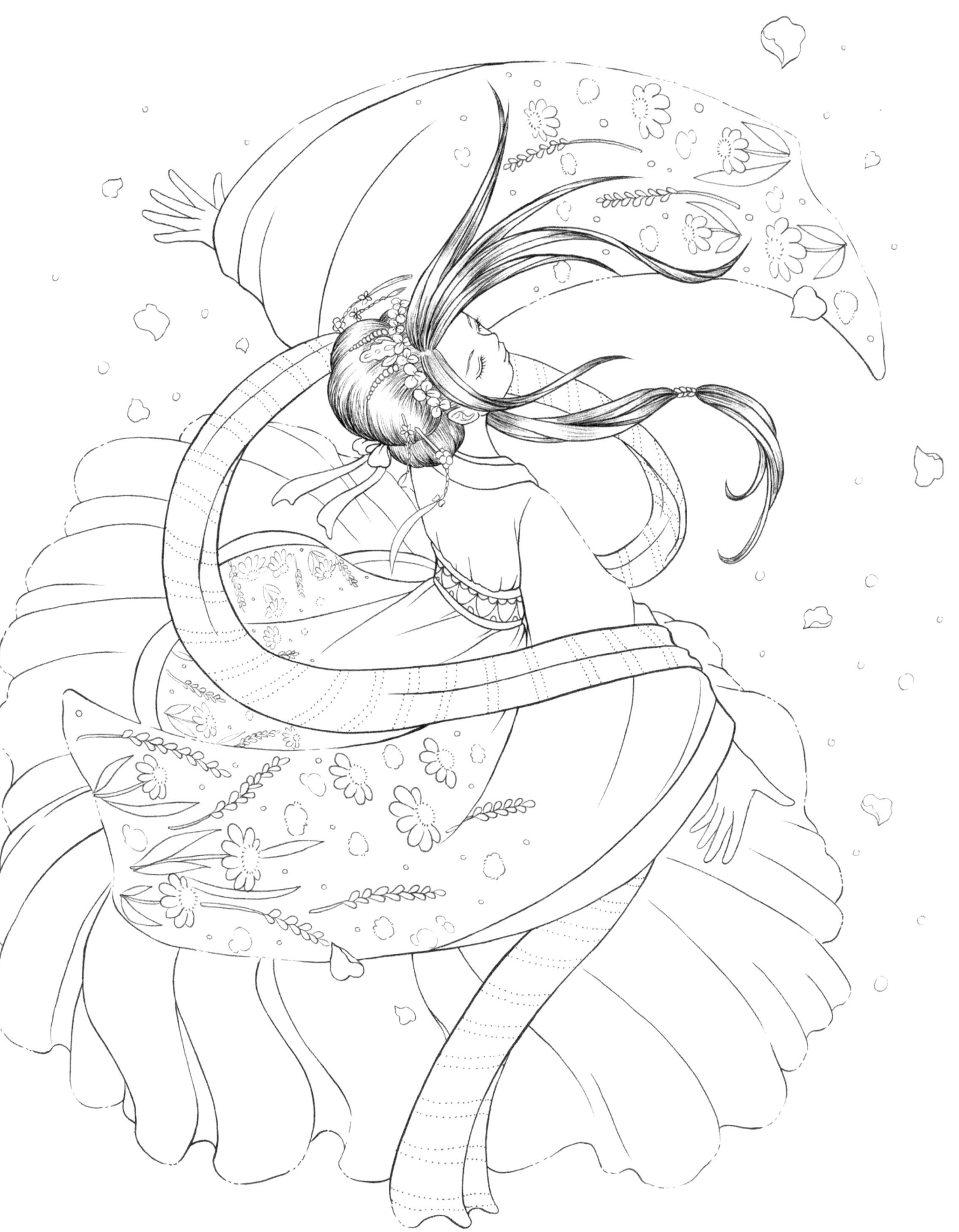

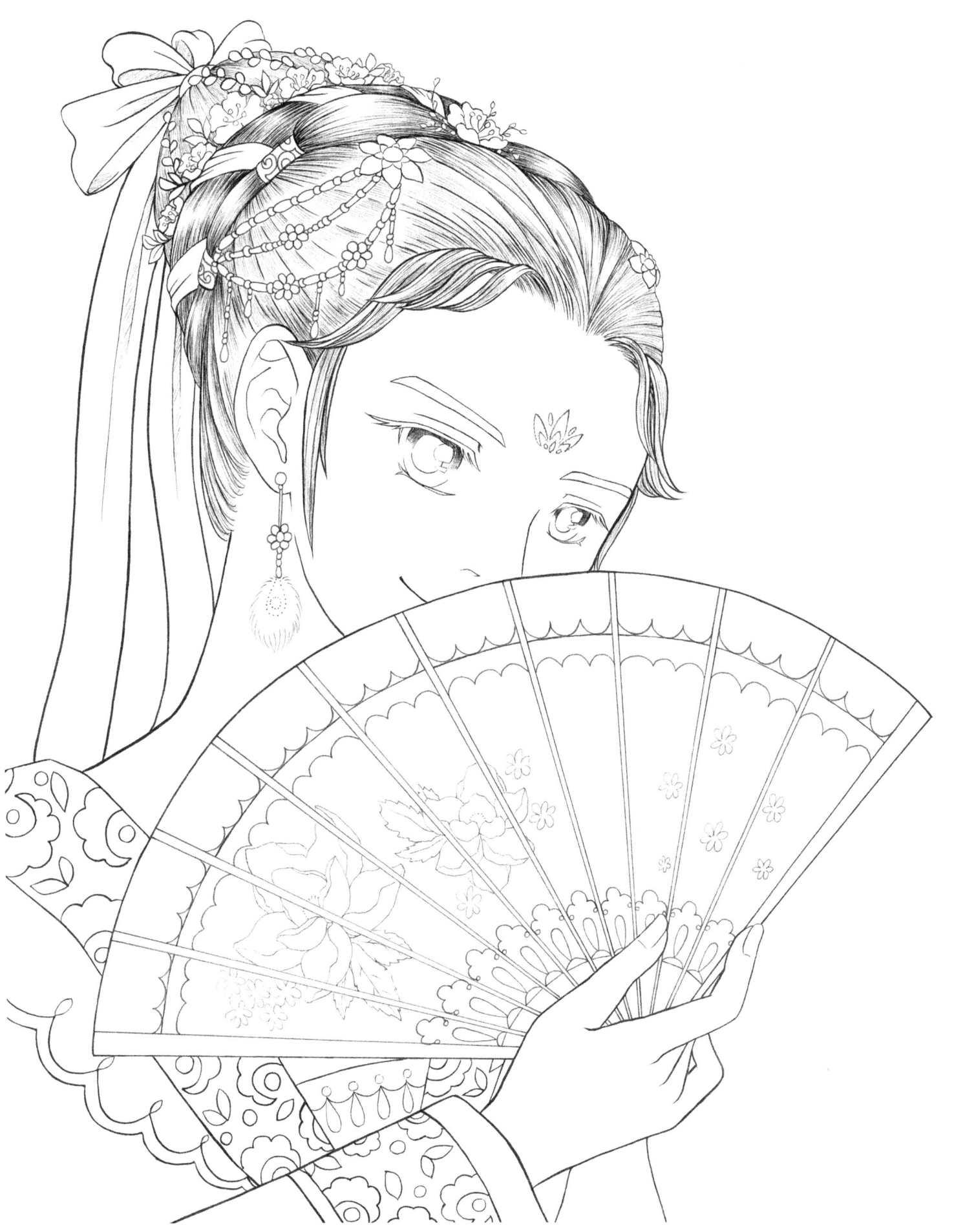

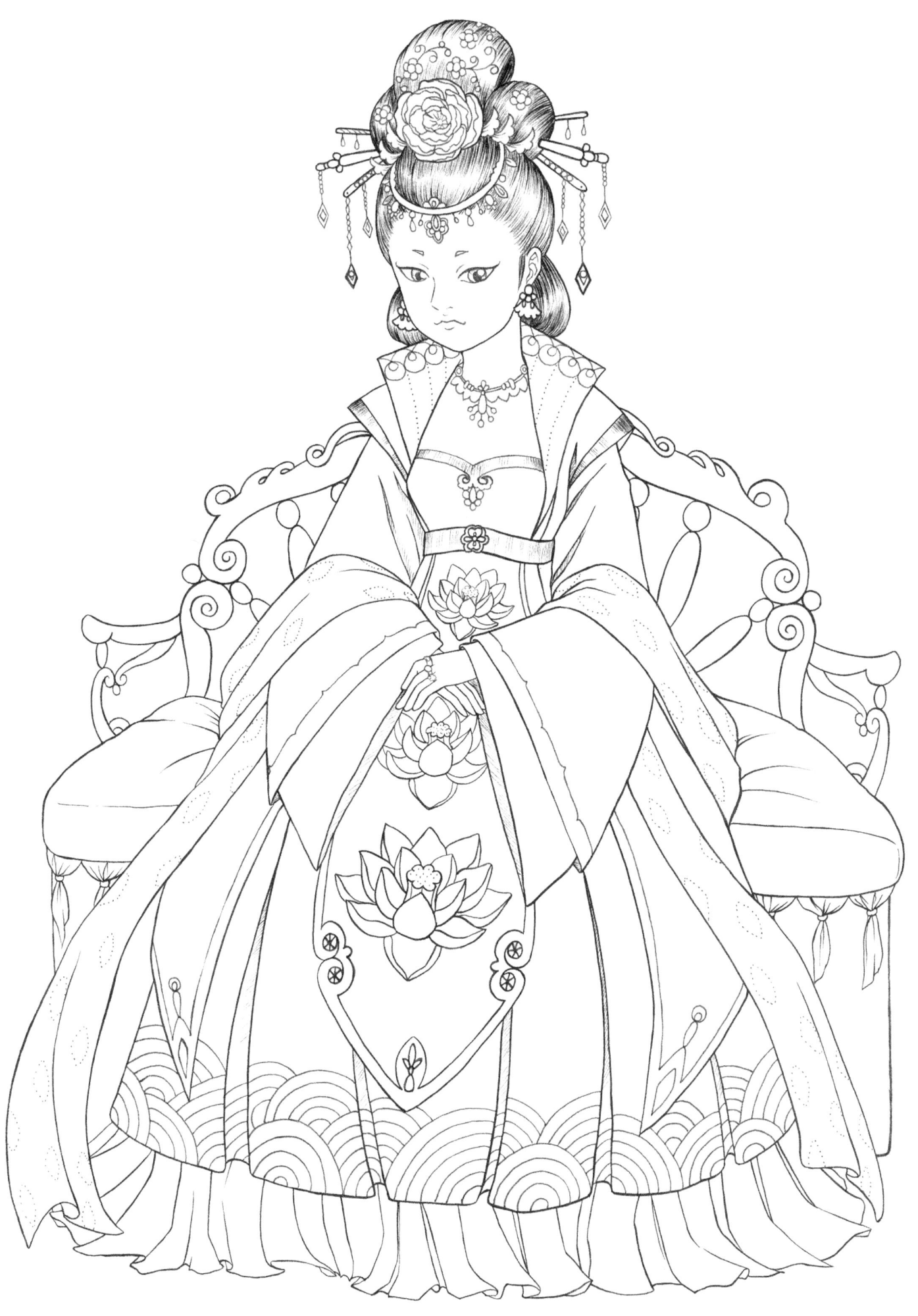

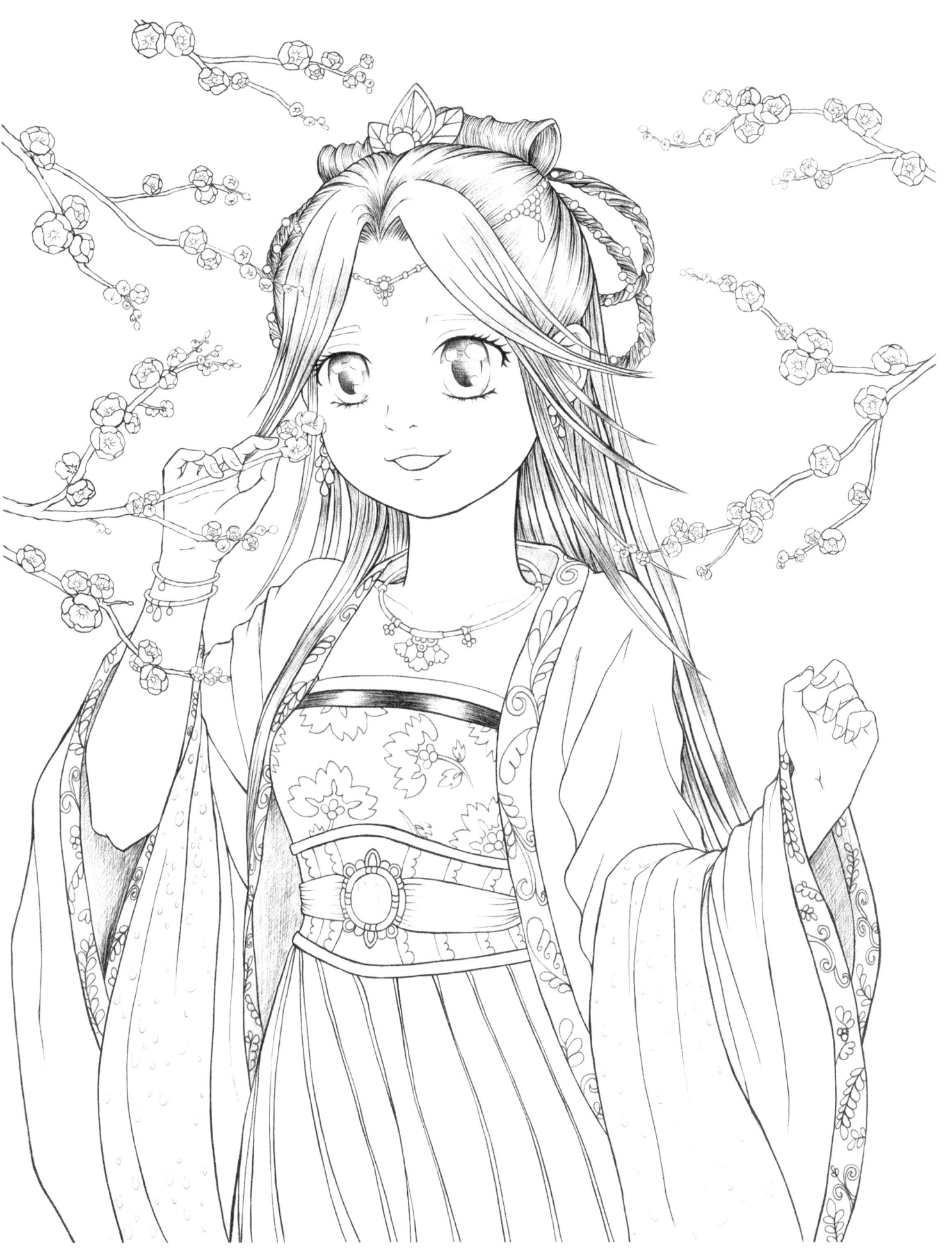

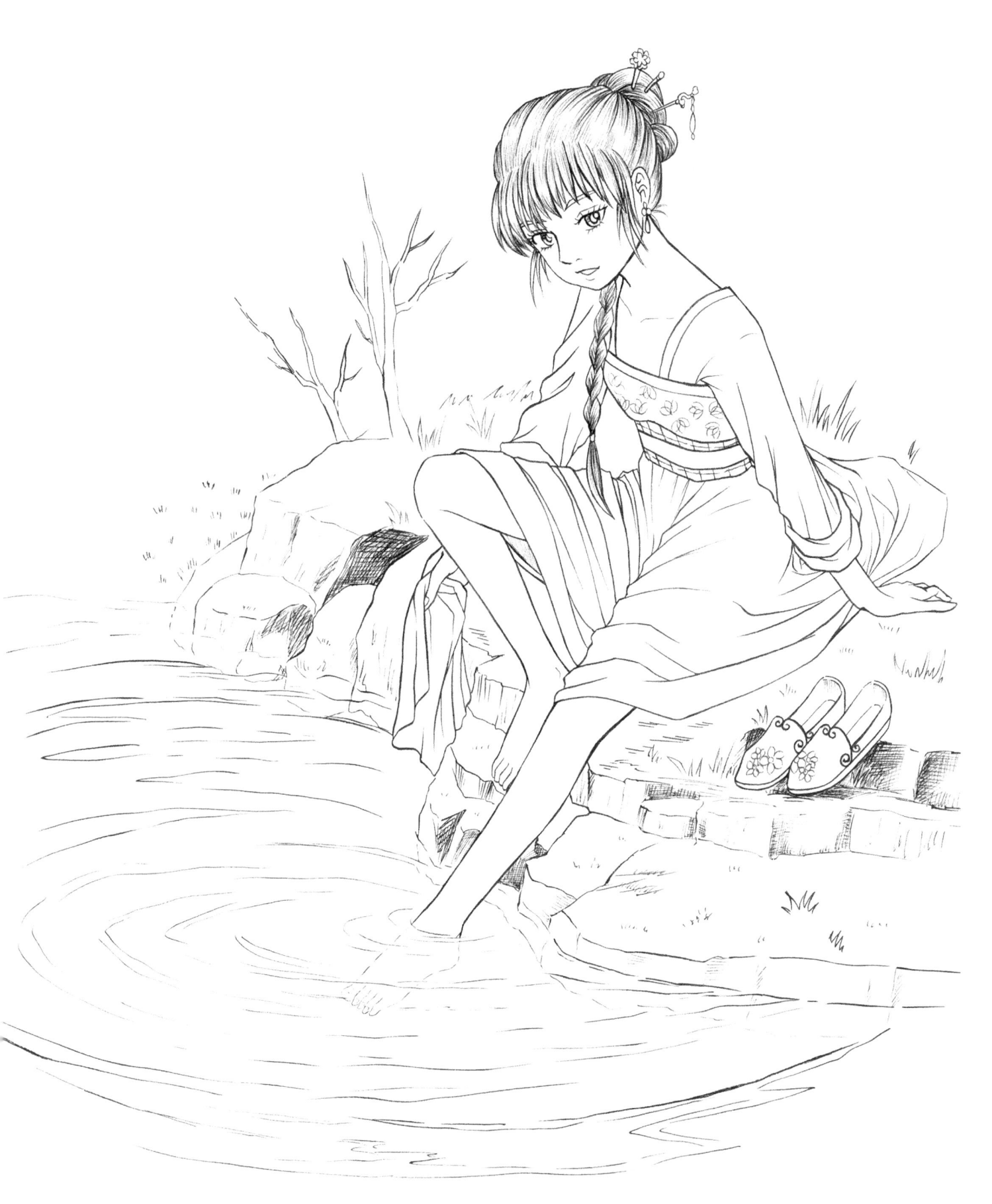

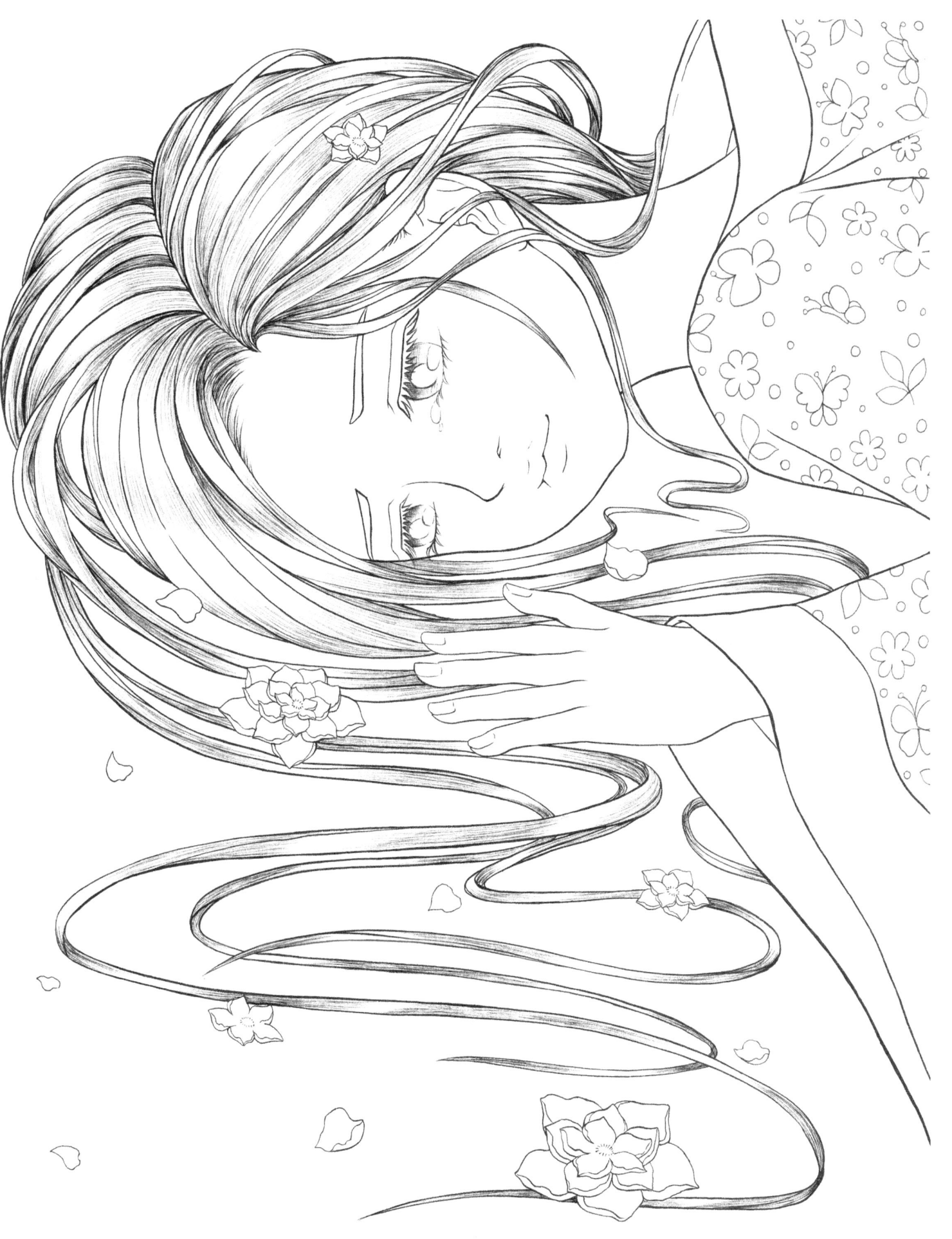

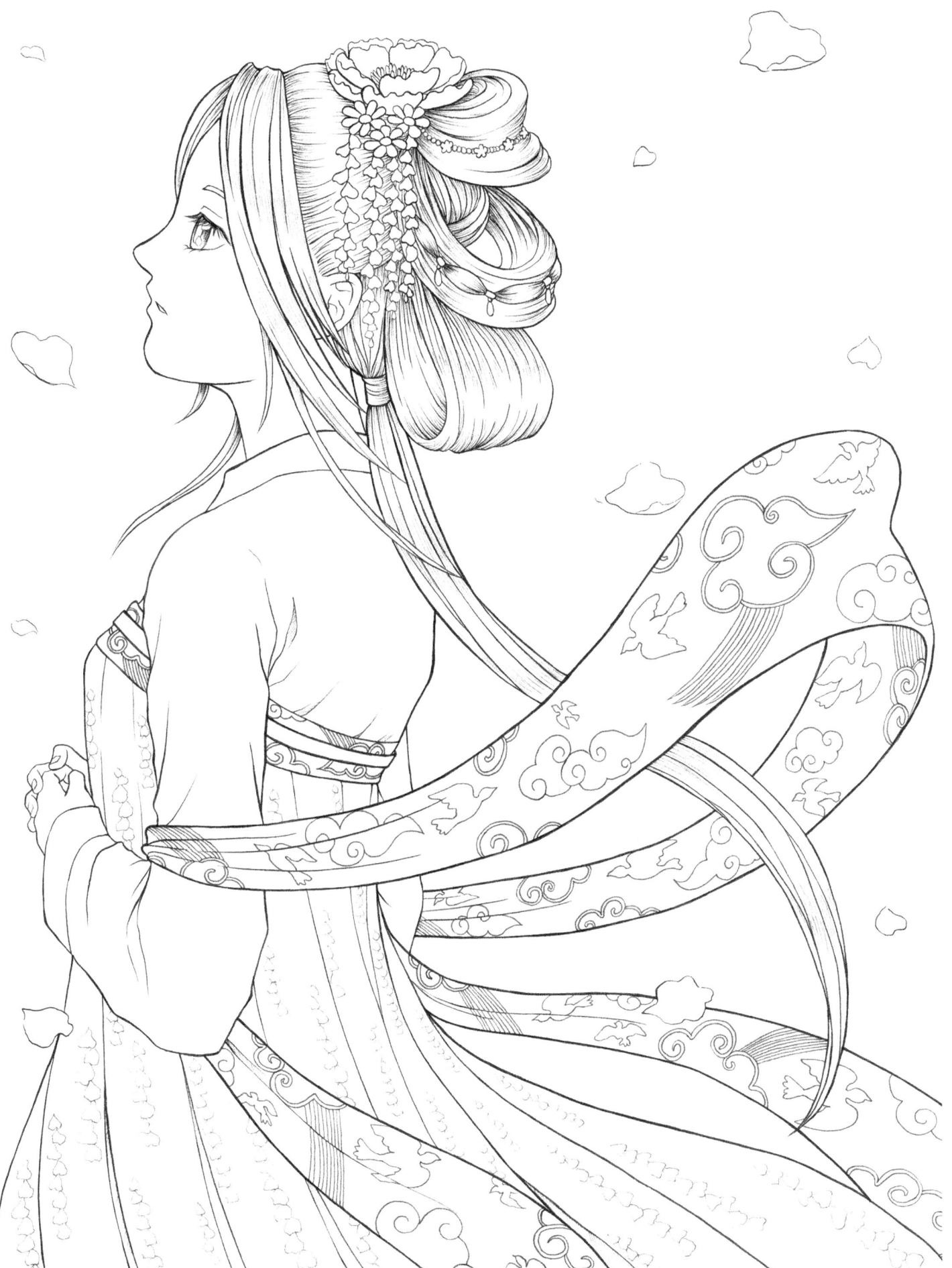

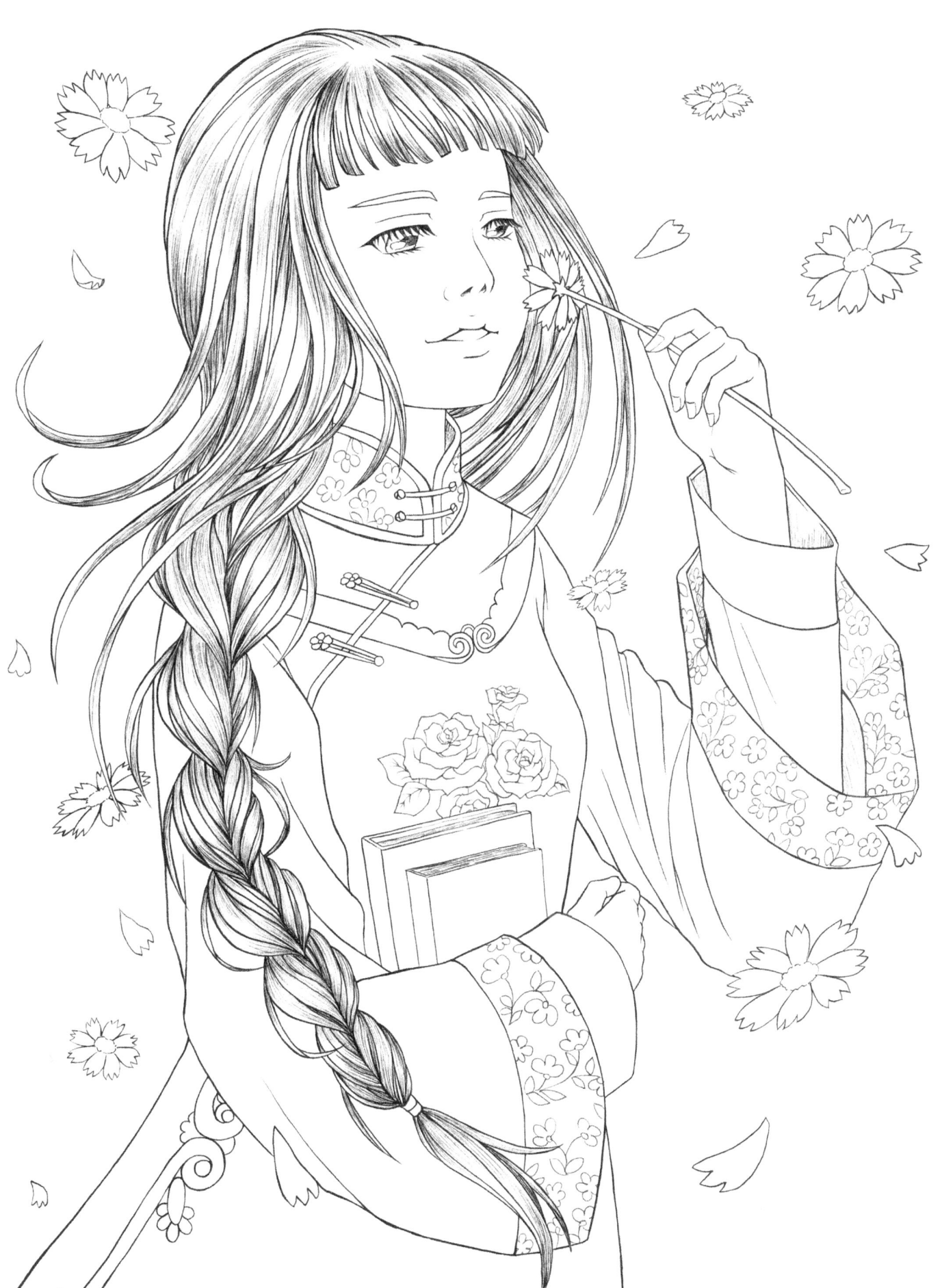

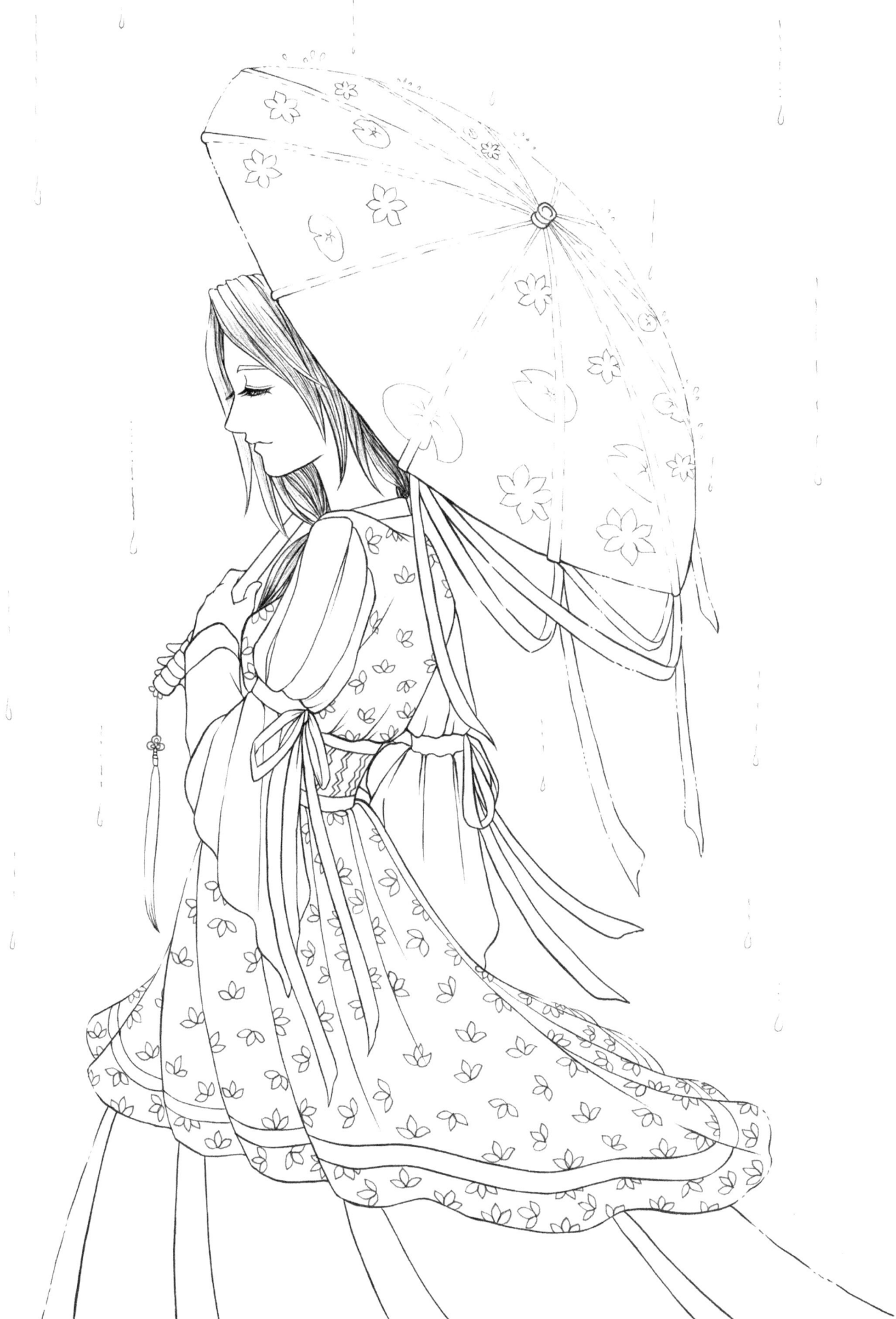

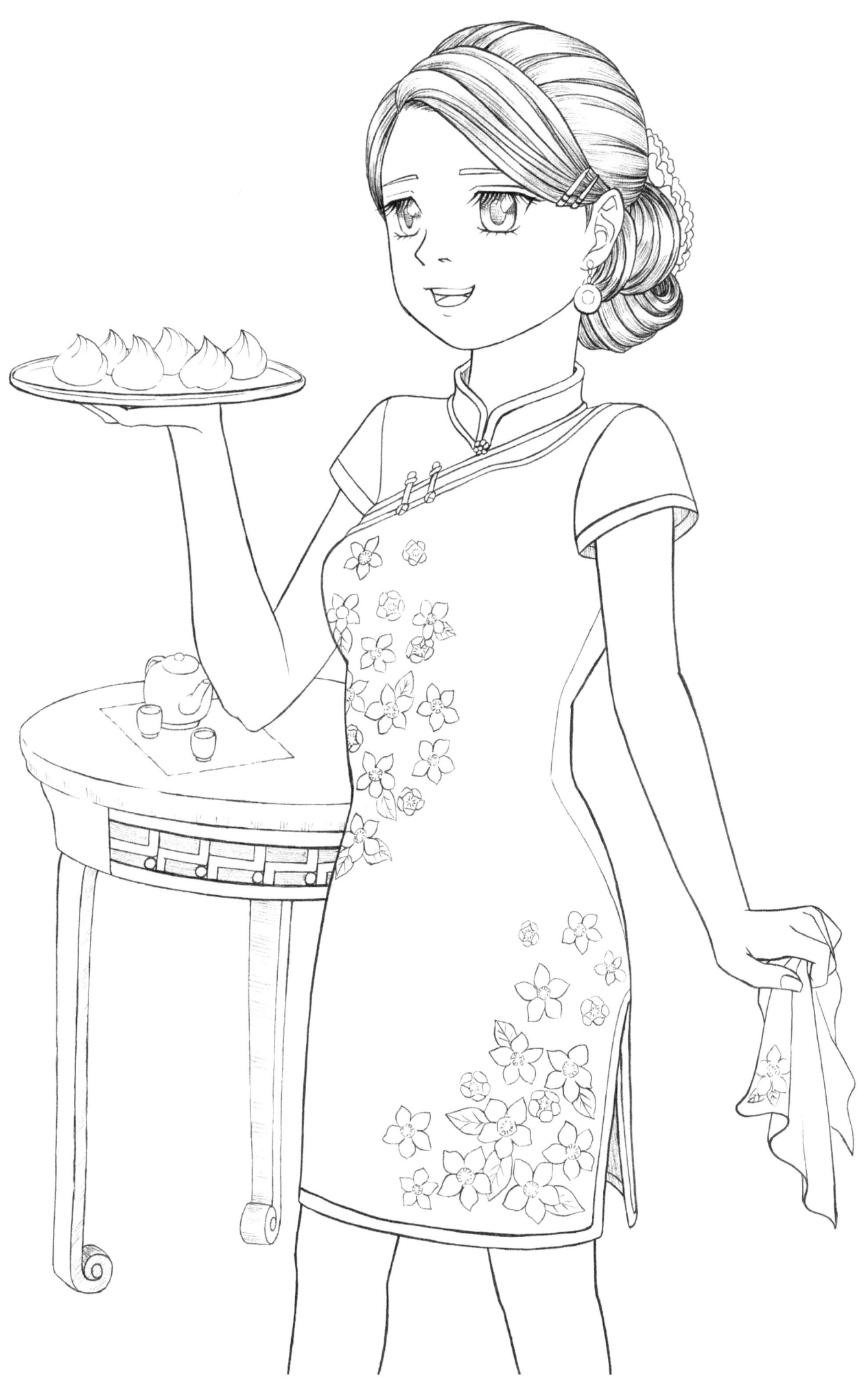

www.ingramcontent.com/pod-product-compliance
Lightning Source LLC
Chambersburg PA
CBHW062337220526
45469CB00008B/2749